COHERENCE
A Practical Guide For Self-Development

Daniel D. Santos

To Lydia, my eternal love and partner in all the adventures that life has presented to us.

To Helena, an angel that came to our family.

To my mom Neusa and dad Jaime, for all the possibilities you opened for me.

And, to my brother Denis and our friendship.

Acknowledgment

This book came to life thanks to the courage and vulnerability that all the coachees and friends I worked with in the past years have demonstrated. Your stories, learnings, and breakdowns are told here. You taught me that we are, truly, much more similar than we think.

Thanks to all those willing to build bridges, respect each other, and walk hand in hand towards the common good.

About the Author

Daniel Santos' career spans 20 years as a Marketing and Sales executive in the Healthcare sector with experience leading teams in Brazil, United Kingdom, and the US. His credentials include a Master in Business Administration by Fundação Instituto de Administração in Sao Paulo, Brazil, a certificate in Positive Psychology by the Oxford University and a business and life coaching certificate by the International Coaching Federation (ICF). Born and raised in Sao Paulo, Brazil, Daniel has been residing since 2016 with his family in New Jersey, US.

www.danieldsantos.com

Contents

Page Left Blank Intentionally

Introduction

We are so different and yet similar at the same time. We all have different ages, ethnicities, were born in different countries, each with its own unique cultures.

Parents, teachers, friends, and life situations all played a role in educating us on how to observe our lives: how to judge, create our "way of being," and the distinctions of what is right and wrong.

But down there, in the moments of suffering, exhaustion, and desperation, we are all very similar.

We all have that inner voice that tells us every day a variation of "Others are better than you," "You are not good enough," "I'm missing out on something," "I need A, B, C to be happy," or "While I don't have this, I won't be fulfilled."

I wrote this book to offer some reflections, questions, and practices.

My role here is not to offer answers. I don't pretend to have the magic formula. Nobody does.

If you came up to read this book, you are curious about your self-development. Most likely, this inner journey started for you many years ago and will continue. I am also in my own journey of learning, making mistakes, feeling miserable and blessed. The fact that I have studied Ontology, Positive Psychology, and practice through my profession, does not make me better than you. In the end, we are on this journey together.

In my own self-discovery process, here are some questions I have been asking:

How can I/we continue the journey of self/others development with more kindness, love, and long term thinking?

How can I/we embrace the idea that our suffering comes from illusions that influence all humankind?

How can I/we separate myself from my illusions, narratives, stories and create space to see new perspectives?

In this book, we will explore how to look at ourselves and others with different eyes, paying attention to things that were always there but we were too busy to notice.

"The real voyage of discovery consists, not in seeking new landscapes, but in having new eyes."- Marcel Proust

A Disclaimer About COACHING

Throughout this book, you will see the word *coaching*, used mostly to describe the work I do on individual and team development interventions.

Over the last years, I have been avoiding this word because it became a label. Unfortunately, a label associated with poor quality work and magic promises to change one's life. If you have any doubts about this, simply look at your social media channels (Instagram, Facebook, Twitter, and others). You will see thousands of "coaching offers" that are nothing but false promises. People who never really did any serious self-awareness work are trying to implement "coaching strategies" on others...

How can I offer something to others that I haven't tried on myself?

Integrity needs to be at the center of the human development coaching process. A good coach will never offer "magic formulas" or claim that he has "all the answers." Neither will position himself as "better" than you because he "knows something that you don't." A good coach will not have the pretension to position himself as a teacher or master.

I am a human being like you – full of light, darkness, possibilities, mistakes, good and bad habits. I have thoughts on my mind that help me achieve what I want and others that limit my potential. I harbor emotions that I want to keep forever and others that I try to avoid at all costs.

I started to study coaching in 2008. Back then, human development coaching was a relatively new area of study, only just starting to flourish and gain space in the mainstream. It was easier to keep the essence and meaning of coaching alive.

At its heart, coaching is a facilitation process conducted by a professional to help others find the answers to what they want to achieve in life. Coaching has nothing to do with providing advice, making people feel better, or giving "solutions" to them.

In such context, this is my invitation to you: to learn what coaching truly implies. Every time you see the word **coaching** in this book, be patient and curious. The real work of a coach and coachee has a deep and sacred meaning.

I am here in this life journey WITH you. To share with but also learn from you. At the end of the book, you will find my contact information. Stay in touch!

Chapter 1
The Big Illusion

I start with one client; a female business executive, mid-thirties, born and raised in the United Kingdom. Her accent is distinct and reminds me of the time I spent working there in 2011. A few weeks later, a second client starts the ontological coaching process with me. He is an American white man, fifty-plus years old, general manager for a mid-size bank. Then others follow: some fellow Brazilians, three Argentinians (two living in Spain), another American. All different people, with contrasting perspectives on how they see the world.

Besides our cultural and language barriers, different stories, careers, different ways of being, we all crave something similar – **Dignity**. We all strive towards accepting the deep reality that WE ARE ENOUGH. The stories I have heard during these initial experiences as a coach are, in essence, very similar to the stories I receive from each client to this day. Deep there in our souls, we are asking for help to find and make peace with our dignity, with the true beauty of life. We are full of light and darkness. We are beginners in some areas of our existence and competent in others. None of us are without our shortcomings – and that's totally ok!

What the Pursuit of Happiness has Produced

As I started to hear the stories my clients were telling me, I was asking myself, *"Where all of this suffering is coming from?"*. The myth of happiness was always there, in the background of the conversation. The desired goals of having a perfect life were the same: happy family, kids, maybe a dog, big house, beautiful furniture, nice cars in the garage. Everything pictured clean and shining, mom and dad looking relaxed, enjoying the moment in their nice clothes and perfect bodies. Yes, like one of those surreal TV commercials. The desire for a perfect life illustrated by these images is so dominant today to the point where it seems to be the ONLY choice we have as we become adults.

Either get a life like this, or you are a loser.

But is pursuing this "happy life" making us happier? Or more miserable?

A happy life translated into MORE usually leads to suffering in the long term. If your meaning for a happy life is more money, material goods, and professional success, you are on the road to becoming financially rich. But, as proven by the chart below, you are not going to be happier.

Figure 7.1: Average Happiness and GDP Per Capita, 1972-2016

Picture 1 – GDP vs. Happiness in the United States. Source: World Happiness Report 2018 - https://worldhappiness.report

Since the 1950s, while the income (blue line) has dramatically increased in the United States (same story for the majority of the world), the happiness (red line) levels have remained flat. Several data sources show that once a person has enough money to afford food, shelter, and other basic life necessities, additional money DOES NOT mean more happiness.

We could debate the happiness vs. income relationship until the end of this book. But I want to offer a different possibility here: what if the problem is not happiness in itself but the definition of happiness?

The materialistic definition of happiness built in the last 300 years (since the Industrial Revolution started) and solidified since the mid-19th century no longer works. Beyond looking at extensive data that proves this conclusion, look at yourself, your family, and friends. We all have much more today than our previous generations.

Access to the internet, smartphones that are mini-supercomputers, smart TVs, the ability to see our friends anytime over video calls, the possibility to study in the best universities of the world from the comfort of your home for free! And much more. All these amazing scientific accomplishments need to be praised. But in itself, they are not enough to create a BETTER life from the point of view of the observer we are. You can have a perfect life on the outside – a lifestyle desired by others. But at the same time, you might be feeling empty, lonely, and stuck. And you are not the only one...

Chapter 2
The Addiction to Productivity

You go to one of your favorite restaurants. As soon as you arrive with your family, there's a table vacant for you — It's your lucky day! The waiter hands you the menus and asks what you want to drink. As the drinks are on the way, you discuss with your wife the options: *should we go with the steak and the pasta for the kids?* After a minute or two, you notice everyone around you is looking at screens: kids on iPads, adults taking photos or scrolling their social feeds. Nobody is talking to each other.

How often has this happened to you? How many times has your own family been on screens when you wanted to have quality time with them?

Modern society continues to push us to produce and consume all the time. *"Why should I lose my time waiting for the waiter to bring the food? I'd better check on my email"*. In addition to happiness narratives discussed on Chapter 1, productivity is another illusion that is creating unprecedented pain in the world.

The internet revolution has brought drastic changes to our society, especially in the last three decades. It has become so easy to work remotely from your smartphone or laptop any time of the day, seven days a week. But as a result, we now often overlook our normal, daily lives to work a "little more" and see a little more of what lies outside of it. The offer to be "plugged" into what is happening in the world all the time through the news is a constant temptation. The apps and their notifications make an irresistible proposal to us every time we unlock our phones: "Look here, you have unread emails. Here's a new Instagram notification. Your friend just sent you an instant message. Don't ignore this discount on offer."

We fall right into the trap and open those notifications, thinking it will not take much longer. However, it always takes long enough to miss out on some actual, human one-to-one interactions or simply disconnect us from the present moment.

Picture 2 – "Look here," the invitation your apps are making all the time

The pandemic of screen addiction is transforming the way we live and not at all in a good way. Look around you and notice what happens at public parks, transportation, or any place where people need to wait for something: people glued to their screens, oblivious to the world around them.

How many opportunities are we missing? Opportunities to say "hello" to each other, to learn something new through others, to even make new friends, or simply look at the sky or landscape around you. But, this addiction doesn't just shut us off from what's around us but also what's inside. With your focus on your phone, you never get the moment to reflect; to notice something in yourself; to pay attention to your thoughts and emotions, resolved or unresolved. Alas, our value has been reduced to how much we can *produce* with our time. As humans and sentient beings, we are much more than this. Our real value resides in who *we are*, not only in *what we do*. This seems like common sense, yet, most of us forget this and keep living, by default, on the "autopilot" mode.

Working 14 hours a day should not be a reason to make you proud—neither the so-called ability to "multi-task." If anything, it should worry you about the time and opportunities you are missing out on, outside of the workplace and work apps.

Saying yes to all the requests is not the standard of competence. It is but a desperate need to please others that you are giving in to. At the same time that you are saying *yes* to others, you might be saying *no* to yourself.

Less Is More

Having to be productive to be 'happy' and having 'value' as a person is another illusion we deal with every day. I, too, was caught in this belief over many years of my life. I started to change when I realized that, in many aspects, doing *less* will actually generate *more* value.

Tired of a never-ending busy routine at work, I started to introduce strategies such as:

- Wait until it is late afternoon to answer the majority of my emails. Therefore, in some situations, the issue is already resolved, and I don't even need to answer. If I do, I answer with enough context and information shared by others (of course, urgent emails I answer right away, but these are few, usually less than ten a day);

- Limit the amount of information I exchanged over instant messaging or apps like WhatsApp: these are only for quick communication. If needed, talk over phone or zoom call;

- Decline my participation in certain meetings where I am not sure of the value I bring. I noticed that, in 75% of these, if I explain why I won't participate, it is totally fine;

These seem like obvious things to do and adopt — in fact, they are — but they are also often missed. They are crucial if one wishes to preserve their health and peace in this fast-paced world.

Everybody talks about doing it, but just a few implement it. Knowing how to set boundaries, *when* and especially *how* to say NO to others, is a skill that is getting more important every day. After all, our value as an individual has no correlation with how much we produce.

Chapter 3
The Infinite Search for Perfection

Imagine hosting a wedding party with 200+ people and trying to make every single guest happy, expecting that, at the end of the party, everyone will say only great things about it. Impossible, right?

In today's world of consumerism and comparison with others, it is so easy to fall into the 'perfectionism trap.' Sure, you can always *have* more and *be* more: money, a bigger house, the latest iPhone, or a Tesla car. You could also be more productive and climb the corporate ladder into the next big job every 18 months – *why wait three years?*

It never ends. For those stuck into perfectionism, the inner stories will always be about "something is missing" or "you need to be better at this or that." It will never satisfy you, even if you achieve it, as you will keep looking for more and more.

"I need to…", "I should have done this…" are also variations of the inner voice of perfectionism. It is an all too common voice nowadays that has also led to unbelievable pain for those who live by it.

Thinking about people I know who are trapped into perfectionism, I would say all of them are "successful." They have great careers, and everyone around them thinks their life is the dream one should follow. However, the constant narrative of "something is missing" makes it impossible for them to celebrate their accomplishments, experience joy, and just live in the present moment. As predicted, they keep looking for more to fill the 'gaps' they feel are howling at them.

I Was Trapped

I was stuck in this trap for many years. I know what it is like working long hours, pleasing my bosses, climbing fast the corporate ladder, and always looking at the top of the mountain. It all started to change when, one day, feeling down and depressed without understanding what was happening to me, I picked up a book called "The Power of Now" by Eckhart Tolle. By sharing his own breakthrough, facing depression, and resigning from a promising job, Eckhart connected deeply with me. His "awakening" to the gift of the present and the practices he offers to live fully in the now are useful to me to this day.

I started to pay more attention to these illusions of Happiness, Productivity, and Perfectionism. They were getting in the way to allow me to have the life I wanted.

The 3 illusions attract each other

The **illusion of perfection** also walks hand in hand with the other two illusions I presented: **happiness** and **productivity**. The search for a perfect, happy, and productive life is the goal for millions of people today. It is a product of this hyper-competitive and consumerist world where a person's value is translated into how much money and success he or she has (or appears to have).

Illusions like those seem so "natural" that those who dare challenge them are labeled as crazy, naïve, liberals, and so on.

But if we stop for a moment, we will notice how blind and immensely constrained we are getting once we embrace the happiness, productivity, and perfectionism as a "way of life."

A few years ago, I was with my daughter at the swimming pool in the condo where we lived in New Jersey. Another child came in and started to play with my daughter. They seemed to be of the same age, about four years old. It didn't take long before I began to talk with the boy's mom. With her being Indian and me a Brazilian, we quickly jumped into a conversation about cultural differences between our countries and the United States.

I was curious to learn more about the Indian culture, giving the fact that I have never been there. One of the points this lady mentioned is how mad she was at her husband. "He keeps putting pressure on our five-year-old boy, saying that he needs to study very hard because in the future he must be admitted at Princeton University." I was shocked. How can a father start putting pressure on his kindergarten school kid, thinking he needs to be "successful enough" to study at Princeton?

Can you imagine what this kid will learn about the meaning of "being a good person"? His entire value as an individual will be limited to his academic performance. And he will most likely follow the steps of a "successful" life: study at one of the best universities in the world, join a large company, make money, buy stuff and sell the same lifestyle to his kids... until, one day, he will ask himself, "what have I done with my life? Why am I so "successful" but I feel so miserable?

Chapter 4
The Third Option

Most people I know — friends, family, company coworkers — are all tired of this "life purpose" translated into illusions like happiness, productivity, and perfectionism.

What About You?

All of these ideas are presented as the desired modes of living, but people know they want something else: a different way to live and appreciate life. Do you also wish for something else besides the clichéd and overly sold concepts of happiness and perfection?

For the majority of us, the answer is yes. But then another question follows: Where to start? How can we aspire to be different when, every time we turn on the internet, TV, radio, or talk to each other, we listen to the same narratives that reinforce the need for more money, success, and fame? A dominant narrative is that, in order to be the way you want, you NEED something. It's a *narrative of lack*. There's a lack of this or that, and as long as you don't have it, you will never be so beautiful, successful, and your life will never be fulfilled. How does one get away from these narratives if they are so deeply entrenched in the world around us?

In the face of this comes a very natural human reaction: *what happens when a person is not satisfied with the reality but doesn't know what to do?*

Some common reactions are:

1. Get pissed off and protest

But to protest against what? If it's not clear, you will find a cause to fight for. It can be politics, the political party A, B, C. The candidate X, Y, Z. It can also be for diversity, environmental protection, or the healthcare system. It can be any one of the many noble causes. But the topic can also be about religion or your football team. Whatever is the reason, there's a risk your relationship with this topic will be very passionate to the point it can make you blind to other perspectives. While protesting for a cause gives you purpose, the passion that supports it might not be the healthiest feeling with respect to your consideration of things that lie outside the cause.

2. Become resigned

A pervasive emotional state found when someone does not accept the reality but also sees no options to get out of that situation is becoming completely resigned. As an example, it is very common to see resigned people in the corporate world. The employee does not like the work, but it needs to be done, and they have bills to pay. So, it's a matter of keeping your head down, staying at the company, and slogging it through your job. But at the cost of a low engagement or even some level of depression. Many people go about life like this, not enjoying what they do for the greater part of the day and moving about like robots.

Look at yourself and the world around you. How many people are either in protest or resignation mode? Are there any doubts that it is the immense majority?

But what about a 3rd option? Is there a way to work against what you do not approve of other than protesting or giving up?

Such an option would allow the person to be dissatisfied but also to focus this energy towards personal and collective expansion, to create new narratives, ways of living together, and cultivate dignity, freedom, and peace.

Beyond words, this is already a reality for many people living in a different emotional state that I call *enthusiasm*.

Embracing enthusiasm is not a rational decision. It can't simply be done by "thinking" about it. Neither is it a magic formula that will solve one's problems. I'm not talking about living in enthusiastic state 24 hours a day – that's impossible. Life will always bring ups and downs.

Nevertheless, there are effective ways to expand our narratives, emotional reactions, and body energy (through sleep habits, eating, body postures) that will put us into a dignified and enthusiastic state. It is what we will start to explore now in the following chapters.

Chapter 5
Embracing the Possibilities

For many years, I lived in a resigned state myself. Having worked for the same company for 20 years, I had professional success (as defined by common sense), but over some years, I had to battle every single day to find and keep the purpose of what I was doing alive. In several moments, I admit that I failed and just lived in the "automatic pilot" mode of productivity, pleasing others and doing my job the best way I could.

The dream of living a different life was always there in my mind, yearning to be manifested. Alas, to get rid of my corporate career seemed too risky, especially now that I was a husband and father; I had to provide a 'good life' to my family. Maybe I just had to accept my life and try to make the best of it, like any other adult.

"Welcome to the adult life," I remember joking with myself as a way to keep going and forgetting any radical plans to change my life.

Yet, it was impossible to forget. I was trying to convince myself every day that I needed to change my life one way or another. Either continue with my corporate career, assume more responsibilities, better benefits, pursue more success and promotions or start something completely new, outside of this world of meetings, politics, and suits.

Then in 2016, my life took on a different direction. After years of planning to live abroad, I moved with my family from Sao Paulo, Brazil, to New Jersey, US. The move was possible because I had accepted a job offer to work in the Global Strategic Marketing team, within the company. Although moving to a different country brought the feeling of starting my life all over again, it still hinted to me a sense of stability, having known the internal processes and how to navigate in the same organization.

Moving to a new country was not something new for me.

I had worked for a year in the United Kingdom back in 2011. But this time, I came to the US as a local employee, and I had no plans of going back to Brazil. My wife was excited; living abroad was her desire since we have had our UK experience a few years earlier.

During the first months in the US, I was also motivated to build a new life. However, as time went by, I started to feel sad and even more resigned than before. I missed my family, friends, Brazil's tropical weather, and the food. Needless to say, it was challenging to adjust for a while.

The internal conversations I was having about continuing with my corporate career or starting something new was also changing. It became clear to me that leaving my corporate career was impossible. *How could I work with something else now that I had a higher cost of living and had to take care of my family in this new country?* It was out of the question. I couldn't put them through difficult times due to my desire to have a different life.

I became increasingly desperate and just did what I do in

these situations: hide these feelings at all costs; fake that all is good; put my head down and work; try to show up at home happy and take care of my family; be a good dad, husband, executive, citizen. But inside, I was feeling a lot of pain, sadness, and resignation. Nowhere to go from here; I felt stuck in a loop with no way out and believed that it was how my life was going to be for years.

It took me a while to understand what was happening to me. I started having panic attacks at work. Those lasted one minute or less, but after the event, I remained worried about what could happen if they returned. *What if I have a panic attack at the next meeting?* I would think, worrying about my health now in addition to my position in life. The two began to worsen each other, and, in the middle was me, not understanding what to do and where to go to change my circumstances.

My life was a mess. I couldn't relax, not even on the weekends. It felt like I was trapped; I was going down a constant downward spiral of mental torment.

COHERENCE

Finally, after a few months, I decided to look for help. It was not easy. *I am an adult, father, husband, man. Why do I need to ask for help? I should be able to solve all my problems by myself* – this was the story going on in my mind on repeat.

At some point, the pain was so unbelievable that it set me free. I decided to be free from this narrative of being a *Superman* that never asks for help. I may be responsible for my family and the people at work, I may have obligations and tasks to oversee, but before all of it, I am a human being with mental and emotional needs. I put aside the view of being invincible and decided to ask for help in order to turn my life and health around.

And I'm so glad I took this step! So many doors were about to open.

Over the next two years, I met amazing people, learned theories that explained my existential crisis, and practices that involved my body, emotions, and mind. I was starting to navigate in a new World of possibilities that allowed me to see so many life choices between the two limited options I had prior created for myself.

Chapter 6
Emotional States

How many opportunities are out there and you are not seeing them?

The opportunities you are too blind to see, others do and take advantage of them.

In my resigned state, I had convinced myself that there were only 2 ways to move forward with my life:

1. Continue in the corporate career until I retire;

2. Get out now, while I was still young. Create a new and totally different career that could inspire me every day.

This very narrow way of seeing my life options was making me miserable. There were in fact thousands, if not millions of possibilities that I could not see. And I was about to discover this as I took a flight in September 2018 and arrived in Boulder, Colorado to start my journey in a development program; it would serve as a retreat and offer me the possibility to become a life and executive coach.

The program transformed my life. The first 6 months were all about myself: my history, why I learned to be the way I was, how I could declare myself a beginner and start to learn to see my life with different eyes.

The simple idea that in order to be a great coach one first needs to be a coachee (the coach's client) is so obvious but unfortunately not followed by many coaches out there. One needs to live the process in himself first to then be able to support other people. It reminds me of the oxygen mask procedure they show in the airplane boarding announcement. You need to first put the mask in yourself to then be able to help the person sitting next to you.

Emotional States

Among the several amazing distinctions and practices that I learned, the emotional states explained A LOT about how I arrived in Boulder.

Emotional states are different from emotions. While the first persist for weeks, months and even years, the latter comes and go easily. If you run for a few miles you are going to feel joy, pleasure. During a busy work day, you may feel impatient, anxious, and angry. But if, in the next day, your agenda is free of meetings and you have enough time for yourself, you will feel a different set of emotions.

Emotional states reflect a person's relation with FACTS and POSSIBILITIES that influence his/her life as illustrated below:

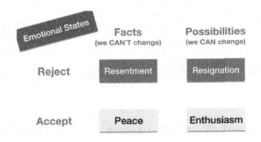

Picture 3 – Emotional States adapted from the work of Julio Olalla and Newfield Network (www.newfieldnetwork.com)

When a person REJECTS the FACTS that influence his/her life, the dominant emotional state will be RESENTMENT. If this rejection is towards the POSSIBILITIES that are available for his/her life, RESIGNATION takes over.

On the other hand, if the person ACCEPTS the FACTS that influence his/her life, the dominant emotional state will be PEACE. If this acceptance is towards the POSSIBILITIES that are presenting to his/her life, ENTHUSIASM (defined as *ambition* by Julio Olalla) takes over.

In Which Emotional State Are You?

Are you carrying on your shoulders the resentment for things that hurt you in the past? Things that might have been absolutely unfair and created an unprecedented level of pain to you.

The past might have been terrible to you, but do you have a time machine to go back and change what happened?

No.

None of us have the means to turn back time, but we have a CHOICE. Either continue to carry this weight on your shoulders, this resentment that affects your health at a bodily, emotional and mental level, or to start to accept what happened and understand that you can be in peace with the things that happened and use this energy towards building a better present and future. Note that I said accept, not agree…

Talking about the present, all of us interact every day with FACTS and POSSIBILITIES. Facts can be proved by science, data. They are not stories, theories or possibilities. If I say that the inflation rate is 5% per year in a particular country, that's a fact. You might not agree with the president or the way the economy has been managed but your opinion is not going to change the fact that the inflation is 5%. You can decide to either be in resentment or peace about this.

POSSIBILITIES are also part of our everyday life. These are stories, narratives, and opportunities. And they can be influenced and changed by us. People that usually are in resentment state towards the FACTS tend to be in RESIGNATION towards the possibilities. This means they don't see the full range of POSSIBILITIES ahead of them at a professional or personal level. They see themselves stuck, limited and with a narrow menu of opportunities in their lives. "My life is boring, repetitive. I don't like my work but I need to pay my bills so I can't quit." That's a common point of view from a person in resignation.

On the other hand, for those who accepted the FACTS and live in PEACE, it's common to find ENTHUSIASM towards the opportunities in life. ENTHUSIASM is much more than just motivation. It is creative energy focused towards a life purpose. It is ambition in the sense of creating new projects, solutions, and conversations. It's about serving others through work or other activities.

Imagine how fantastic your team, family, town, country and our whole world will be when the immense majority of the humanity learns how to live in an emotional state that involves PEACE and ENTHUSIASM?

Chapter 7
Attention as the First Step

Forget the 10 steps to live in PEACE and ENTHUSIASM. There is no magic formula to shift your emotional states. Understanding and feeling the emotions in your body, paying attention to your energy levels and stories that go on in your head takes a lot of commitment. It is a journey, a marathon, not a 100-meter sprint race.

Accepting that ups and downs created by emotions and moods are part of life relieves the pressure for results in the time being. Simply embrace the reality that all emotional states (even resentment and resignation) have a purpose: to ask you to pay attention to areas of your life that you have been neglecting. To take action and change the course of your destiny is another vital purpose.

Here is a list of effective practices to start noticing your emotional states (also known as moods). To perceive what is happening with you is the first step towards the "shift":

1. Pay attention to your emotions. Don't judge; do not hold yourself to standards of perfection by feeling guilty about having a particular emotion. Just be there and honor the emotion you are feeling;

2. Have a journal (preferably paper and pen instead of smartphones) to take notes on what you are feeling and which insights are coming to you;

3. Avoid multi-tasking. Do one thing at a time. This will enhance the attention to your feelings and the thoughts behind those. For example: "I noticed that I'm feeling anxious this morning. And I wonder if the story behind my anxiety is that is impossible to complete this project at the deadline."

<u>The emotional state you are will be the lens through how you see the life around you.</u>

If you are living in enthusiasm, you will see possibilities and most of the time, the glass will be half full. You will have an impulse to reach out to others and co-create this new future for your life in the form of projects and initiatives.

You will feel that it is time to allow your dreams to manifest themselves and come true. On the contrary, for those living in resignation, everything that happens "outside" will look simply more or less the same, for they live a routine where possibilities are limited. "Why should I start this new project if I know the chances of being successful are minimal?" they will often think.

The Value of Shifting your Emotional State

Think about the new opportunities you will take advantage of, how much your business will expand, how many amazing people you will come to know, and the new exciting things you will learn, all BECAUSE you are in an emotional state of ENTHUSIASM.

Enthusiasm has this energy of being open to possibilities, but it is also more than that. It also allows the opening of options in life that are aligned with your life purpose, with being a person who will serve others. This is a key distinction between enthusiasm and excitement. Enthusiasm is energy focused through one's purpose and

41

vision, while excitement is motivation without focus. We will detail the practices to shift your emotional states in the next chapters, but it's important to note that, on a deeper level, shifting emotional states requires working at three key domains of life:

Mind

Your thoughts, stories and narratives make up the domain of your mind. What is said to others and what you keep to yourself plays a big role. The external and internal conversations have an impact on the shift of your emotional states.

Emotions

Every emotion can come and go within minutes but it can also become, over time, a mood or emotional state. Therefore, knowing your emotions, paying attention to those and being able not only to accept and honor but also shape your emotions is a key practice.

Body

Your bodily energy, health, the way you walk, talk, how your body shows up in meetings or when you are with family or friends is important.

Work done on these three levels or domains of life will result in a consistent shift in emotional states.

Chapter 8
Change or Expand?

Change implies there is something wrong: something that needs to be replaced, forgotten, avoided, or removed from existence.

I understand the value of embracing change when we are talking about a business plan, strategic priorities, or tactics to drive a business. But when it comes to people development, the pursuit of change creates enormous levels of pain and is mostly ineffective. Think about the feedback sessions you had. Whether you gave or received feedback, what happened during the conversation when the topic of CHANGE came to the table? What happened when someone told you to be perhaps not the way you are? Were your feelings towards this comment positive at all? We can always try to embrace change at a personal level. However, frustration and resignation tend to dominate our emotions and create narratives that limit our achievements.

Are you familiar with these narratives? Have you been telling this to yourself too?

"I will never change. I'm too old."

"I tried to lose weight for the past ten years. Forget it. I'm done."

"My boss is always asking me to change. This sucks. I give my best every single day at work and can't change what he/she wants. I will never be like that."

The Power of Expansion

Expansion brings a different distinction. It does not imply that there's something wrong inherently. Therefore, expansion frees one's inner energy (physical, emotional, and mental) to develop new competencies and learn in new areas of life. To begin seeing life in a broader way is the goal.

Moreover, expansion isn't limiting; it does not mean we

need to choose one way or another. You can continue to embrace the qualities and strengths developed in your life, the areas where you are competent or even an expert. And, at the same time, you can declare yourself a beginner in areas of life that are new to you.

At 38 years old, I started to play tennis. I was a beginner. I could barely hit the balls. In my first classes, I felt terrible. *I'm too old for this. I will never learn*, I used to think. But guess what started to happen after 3-4 classes? I got better. I began to enjoy the game.

It's ok to be a beginner.

Why do I need to call myself a loser every time I commit a mistake while learning?

I have more than 20 years' experience as a business executive in Marketing and Sales. In some domains, I am competent and, in others, an expert. In cooking, with anything beyond pasta and very simple dishes, I am a total beginner. I accept this fact because the life I had so far didn't allow me to become an advanced beginner or competent cook. If I want, I can still look for ways to expand myself in this life domain.

Expansion is about accepting where you stand and permitting yourself to go beyond that. It is all about exploring new spaces in your life while taking advantage of the areas you are already comfortable in. While change demands a complete renewal, expansions make you build upon your pre-existing qualities.

The next time you see someone talking with you about a habit or characteristic that this person does not like in him/herself, pay attention to how much pain the "I can't change story" is creating. Then recommend expanding those qualities that they already possess, and their outlook will flourish.

How about you offer this person the gift of allowing him/herself the belief of expansion instead of change?

As for myself, I only started to notice the impact of the "need to change" pressure on my life when I was 28 years old.

Chapter 9
A New Way to Look
at my Life

A crisis hit my life when I was about 28. On the surface, I was a successful Marketing Executive, recently married to the love of my life, living in a pleasant apartment in one of the best neighborhoods of Sao Paulo, Brazil's financial capital.

But, behind the appearances, I was desperate for change. *"It's time to resign from this company, live in another country, do a master's degree. If I don't act now, I will get stuck into this life forever"*, I used to say to myself.

In my search for a way out, I stumbled upon the Digital Nomad Movement. Life should be designed, not lived by default. One could learn to live with less money without compromising lifestyle by moving to countries like Thailand, where the cost of living was cheap compared to Sao Paulo or any other major world city. The digital nomad could work from any country, using no more than a good laptop and an internet connection. Think about yourself working a few hours a day in Thailand, having free time during the rest of it to go to the beach. Enjoying life, living fully with zero stress – I was caught into this dream.

I know people that implemented this plan and were successful. But how many tried and never achieved their dream? More than going to Thailand or any other exotic country with beautiful beaches, sunny weather, and low cost of living, how many people CONTINUE TO BE HAPPY after the dream comes true?

This formula can work for some, but not for all. The problem of the "magic formula" approach that the digital nomad movement sold is to believe this way of living is a solution for everyone. This oversimplification mostly brings frustration, and people return to their "old lives" after a few months "living the dream."

Looking for Help

Although I was very tempted by the Thailand dream, I decided I had to share my crisis with people that could help me see other perspectives. Was I blind? Becoming a digital nomad was the only way to go? I needed to test my hypothesis. I remembered that when I was in my early 20s, I had read something about life being divided into cycles of 7 years.

Each new cycle (I was 28 now) offered a life crisis that could eventually be turned into an opportunity to revisit the meaning of one's life, values, and goals for the years to come. Connecting the dots and finding out more about this theory, I started doing psychotherapy sessions under the Anthroposophy method called Life Biography.

The sessions seemed like a regular therapy conversation but guided by the 7-year cycle framework. From 0 to 7 years old, we are physically born, our main development being the physical body and getting to know the world around us. From 7 to 14, the development starts at an emotional level. From 14 to 21, the years of our adolescence, rational development takes place, which triggers questions about who we are, what is our place in the world, why the world works in a particular way, and so on. From 21 to 28, we become adults, and our body, emotions, and mental skills develop even more. At 28, another cycle starts and offers new challenges: you are now a fully grown adult. Key questions emerging at this phase are:

Which type of life do I want to have?

What is the meaning of life after all?

HOW do I want to live; what is important to me?

One Insight that Changed Everything

After months of Biography sessions, I came to a simple but powerful insight: what if the solution is not moving to a new country, having a new career, and radically changing my entire life? What if what is limiting me is THE WAY I SEE my life?

I eventually lived with this premise for the upcoming years. I continued with my corporate career, and even without knowing the distinction between CHANGE versus EXPANSION, my life became lighter – less stress, more joy.

From time to time, the temptation to follow the Digital Nomad or another movement came back. This usually resulted in a lot of daydreaming, took energy and motivation from the present moment to bet in a future that never came.

Looking back, I accept that I just acted with the knowledge and emotional structure that I had at that time. But, if I could go back in time, I would definitely say to myself: "stop daydreaming and start paying attention to the possibilities that are around you, every single day."

A Model

I only fully understood the pain I was self-inflicting and how to get out of these mind traps when I started my ontological coach journey years later.

Ontology is the study of the being. *Why do you act, feel and see the world in a certain way?* – this is a question that lies at the heart of ontology.

While a regular coach will help its clients better define what they want and design an effective action plan to get there, an ontological coach will go further—starting with how does the client sees his/her life. Why? Where does this "way of seeing the world" come from?

This model, called OBSERVER, ACTION, and RESULTS (OAR), changed my life and made me understand the crisis I described.

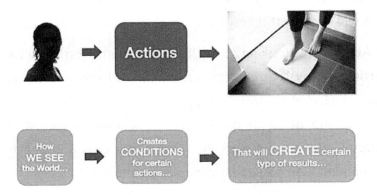

Picture 4 – Let's say your objective is to lose weight. Before we start with the actions that will drive this goal, we need to explore you do you see your body and your relationship with weight.

The way you see your life is going to create a menu of options (actions) that will produce certain types of results. See your life in a limited way, and your actions will be limited and repetitive too. And, if the actions are always the same, guess what will happen with the results?

Before helping the client create the actions that will produce the results he/she wants, the ontological coach will <u>understand the observer that this client is</u>. This will be the starting point. Expand the observer you are, and you will be expanding the possibilities of actions you can take that will drive better results.

At 28, I was looking at my life with resignation and in a particular way that created such a limited set of actions. Those included essentially staying on my corporate career forever and dying of boredom or becoming a free and happy digital nomad working in front of a beautiful beach in Thailand. Can you guess which one I chose?

Chapter 10
A Transformational
Approach

At this point, you might be thinking: "This is interesting, but how can I observe my life in a different way? How can I start paying attention to the opportunities coming my way? How can I achieve the results I want to see in my personal and professional life?"

Here is where I start my work as an ontological coach. Looking at the observer that my clients (individual or teams) are, I assess what thoughts and narratives they have, what their emotional state is, and in which ways all of this is translated into how their body reacts.

In the following picture, you can see the summary of this transformational approach:

Observer - Action - Results (OAR Model)

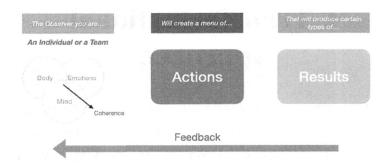

Picture 5 – OAR model overview (Adapted from Newfield Network US)

Through life and its experiences, you developed a certain perspective in how you view the world. This development was influenced by your culture, parents, teachers, childhood friends, and situations you had to deal with.

If someone is born in the United States, there is a natural tendency to "see" the world in a significantly different way than, say, people born in Japan. Alternatively, to present a more extreme example, think of a 30-year-old woman born and raised in Afghanistan. How do you think this person sees her life, role as a mother, wife and career perspectives in comparison to, say, a native French woman?

When we become adults, we take for granted the belief that our way of observing life is the correct one. We will most likely only question ourselves in moments of crisis (this is when we see how a crisis can actually be a blessing).

This particular way of observing our life does and will create a broad or limited menu of options. Actions we can take in each domain of our routine: professional decisions, family, and personal choices, all will be either broadened or limited, depending on our perspectives. These actions can be as small as choosing a restaurant or as impactful as deciding to resign from your job to move to another company.

The menu of actions you use will create results. If these are effective, considering the standards you have for yourself, the feedback loop will tell you to continue to do the same. But if, at some point, the results no longer work for you, what do you do? Here lies one of the critical distinctions between ontological and "regular" coaching. In moments of crisis, a regular coach will bring you back to revisit your actions. If the results you are having no longer work, you should change your actions. That's the belief.

But what if the actions you need to take are beyond your menu of options? For example, if Mary is extremely shy, how can I ask her to make not one but dozens of presentations to customers over the next two weeks? She might be able to do it strenuously, but at what personal cost? Over-preparation, stress, panic attacks?

This is one of the reasons why, in ontological coaching, instead of revisiting the actions, we need to look back at the observer.

Let's say that John is a talented finance analyst. He is making rapid progress in his career. Extremely committed, he always over-delivers in terms of quality and closing his projects before the deadline. As expected, John is promoted to a manager position, but now he needs to lead a team of three finance analysts. Within six months on the job, his performance is average, his self-confidence is gone, and he does not know what is happening... John is stuck into the belief that being a great professional is to deliver projects with quality and on time. This type of action produced the result he wanted: the promotion to his next career step. But now, he needs to embrace actions that will align with the demands of a managerial position.

As an observer, John learned that life is a competition. Only the best ones will survive. His dad was a semi-professional athlete and pushed him to compete since he was a kid. Now, at 25 years old, engaged, recently promoted, and with an immense pressure he puts on his shoulders to "be successful" at work, John feels hopeless.

The way he is observing life (as a competition) does not allow him to act as a leader that listens to and empowers his team, someone who knows how to share his work, co-create instead of lead all the time. He does not have these "options" in his menu of actions. To truly support John, as a coach, I would need to go back to the observer he is.

Together, with John in the "driver's seat", we will understand why he learned to see his life through the lens of competition, what are the benefits and downsides of this way of looking, and how to expand himself as an OBSERVER. From there, new actions will be available to him that will eventually generate unprecedented results.

Chapter 11
The Coherence "Magic"

Think about a situation where you saw someone making a speech: a celebrity, a senior leader at your work, someone defending a proposal to implement a project, or offering a different perspective on a particular subject.

Now think about a presenter who managed to convince you versus a person who did neither engaged or changed your beliefs at all. What is the difference between the two? What made you believe?

Of course, the circumstances of the speech, the topic, and your identification with the presenter all have a role in making you believe in or ignore one's arguments.

But there is something more… though difficult to explain, it is "something" that certain people have, and it makes us believe in them. Authenticity, dignity, honesty: this "quality" has so many names. Among all, I usually refer to it as COHERENCE.

When we *say* something *aligned* with our beliefs, emotions, and motivations, we have COHERENCE in our speech and argument. It is the same "magic" the person that convinced you was using.

But how many times are we truly living in and talking through Coherence?

A Historical Perspective

In the last 400 years, we have seen unbelievable progress in science, industry, and technology. This process began with the Industrial Revolution that took place in Europe in the mid-17th century, later expanded into the US, and has now spread to the whole world.

The belief system that sustained this movement started with the Age of Enlightenment in Europe. Science and religion became two different (and often opposed) perspectives. A man and his mind were no longer made to serve God. Instead, mankind was now taking charge and perceived itself to be able to change the world through rationalism. The belief in dominating nature simply to extract resources and drive industrial production was widespread. The rational mind could create technology, organize and increase production by structuring an economic system based on the ideals of Capitalism.

This new Era has brought enormous improvements to our living standards, such as doubling the individual life expectancy (from 40 to 80 years old), offering high-speed communication systems, allowing new ways of working, living and being, and much more.

But now, several years into the 21st century, there is a clear need for a new way of life. The beliefs that sustained the Age of Enlightenment are no longer enough for the current times.

New Beliefs

How many times have you measured your life and lived by the constraints of these two narratives?

1. "Your thoughts are more important than your emotions. Think, and you will find the solutions."

2. "Your value as a person resides in your professional success and in how much you work (produce), the amount of money you make, and status you have."

These are just two examples of beliefs that created the conditions for the Age of Enlightenment and the Industrial Revolution.

Like all BELIEFS, these two also work in order to drive certain types of results. If the desired result is to increase productivity, production, and Gross Domestic Product (GDP), the beliefs above will be extremely useful...

But what if the desired result is to live with more meaning, inner peace, and emotion-body-mind Coherence? In this case, we need to start to develop new beliefs.

For example, the following:

1. "Your emotions are as important as your thoughts."

2. "Your value resides in your Dignity and Self-Love."

When a person embraces beliefs like these, the path to Coherence between what he/she feels, thinks, and does is wide open.

Coherence is the "magic" that will allow anyone to live in a state of peace, joy, freedom, and ambition. It is a magic potion available to all of us...

PART 2
Where to Start?

"Where do I start to find my "magic", the Coherence that will drive a different way of life?" You might ask.

In my experience, although our natural instinct is to start with the mind by revisiting our beliefs, the most effective transformation happens when we start with mind, body, and emotional practices combined. The risk of putting too much emphasis on the mind alone is to get stuck into thoughts; overthinking instead of jumping into action. Think too much, and you will find more thoughts and considerations. It is a repetitive cycle.

Therefore, in this second part of the book, I want to offer practices that will involve the body, emotions, and mind to create an effective cycle of expansion, allowing you and those around you to live in Coherence.

Ontological development is transformational at an

individual and collective level, in both personal and professional domains, but practice needs to be constant to attain results.

In this part, you will find practices that I have implemented in myself and my clients. My invitation is that you bring these practices to your daily life with curiosity and open spirit. Moreover, start to design your own practices. Once you have understood the ontological framework discussed in Part 1, you will be able to customize exercises to deal with specific breakdowns you are having and even create interventions that will support the development of others around you.

Chapter 12
Declarations

Declaring is one of the most fundamental practices that transformed the way I looked at my life.

A Declaration can be made by a group of individuals (think about the United States Declaration of Independence), an organization (a company mission, a public statement, the announcement of plans for the future), or even an individual. When we declare something, we start to create conditions for the desired future to become a reality. We are allowing (and preparing for) future plans, goals and such to become a reality.

Declarations can be shared with others or kept to yourself. When shared, you create a commitment to what has been said with others. For example, if I declare to my wife that I will lose 10 pounds in the next three months, this shared declaration is also a commitment to her and me. However, in some cases, you might want to keep the declaration to yourself due to confidentiality or other personal reasons. Such declarations can be equally powerful since you are creating a commitment with yourself.

An Example

What I usually recommend to my clients are the following steps:

1. Write down a few paragraphs stating in full detail your declaration. Use words that will engage you – ones that will touch your heart and energize you to overcome the challenge you are facing;

2. Repeat your declaration every morning before you start your activities (work, house tasks, leisure etc.);

3. Audibly speak out the words while standing up (preferably). Feel the declaration in your body as you speak. Just pay attention to your body, energy and emotions as you make your declaration. Don't judge or overthink;

4. Repeat this exercise daily for at least one month. Note down the insights you have during or after the declaration in your journal;

5. As the days go by, if the declaration starts to become "automatic" and thus, lose its impact, consider changing the words or even entire sentences. Incorporate new content that will speak to your emotions.

Below is one example of a declaration. Let's assume this person has a need for developing his/her dignity and self-love:

"I love myself for who I am: a human being full of light and darkness.

I allow myself to be a beginner in the areas of life that are new to me.

I allow myself to learn, make mistakes and ask for help.

It's ok to be a beginner. It's ok to learn and to make mistakes.

I also allow myself to be an expert in the areas of life that are familiar to me.

In those areas, I manifest the qualities I have and put those qualities to serve others and the world around me.

I am open to the millions of opportunities that life offers to me daily.

I am open to learning new experiences. And through the knowledge I acquire, creating a better future with others.

I allow myself to live fully in the present moment, with Dignity and Freedom.

Thanks."

To share my own experience, once I started practicing my declaration, I never stopped. In fact, it became part of my routine, as habitual as eating a meal every day. Though, one thing I still pay special attention to is whether the declaration has been effective or has just become an activity I do in the "automatic pilot." If the latter is the case,

I usually change parts of the declaration or even the body posture in which I speak.

Chapter 13
Facts versus Stories

What do you think is the difference between these two statements below?

- "I was not promoted in the last 36 months."

- "There's no way I will be promoted here."

It seems obvious that the first is a **fact** and the second is a **story**. It may be fully apparent, but when it comes to real life, we tend to mix facts with stories all the time.

Let's look at the following:

- "I don't have time to take care of myself."

- "I need to please others; otherwise, people will not like me."

- "I am not good at sports."

- "I always had trouble finding the right partner. I don't think I will ever find a true love."

All are stories I heard from clients, friends, family members and even myself. Stories that have been with these people for so long, they started to believe as if they were the reality. The *way things are* or facts.

But these examples are not facts. They are stories, (sometimes also referred to as beliefs and narratives)

We all, as human beings, are story makers – to create stories, meaning and culture is what makes us different from animals. In fact, it is the trait of ours that predate even written languages. Tens of thousands of years ago, we were already creating stories and expressing them through artwork in the caverns where we lived.

Picture 6 – Thousands of years ago, we already created stories. The oldest cave art dates back to 45,000 BC. For comparison, it wasn't until 3,500 BC that the first written language emerged.

Similar to emotions, stories are not necessarily good or bad. They just are what you make them to be.

One meaningful way to look at the stories you created for yourself is to ask this question: **do they help you to achieve the results you want?**

If the answer is yes, no problem. Keep going and use the power of the stories you have about yourself, others, work, family, your place in the world and more.

But usually, when we ask such a question, it's because the current stories are no longer working, and we need to open space for different stories. Everyone will deal with life events that require new stories. For example, when I was a teenager, my stories about fatherhood were very different from the stories I created (or took from others) when I actually became a father. I needed new stories at that time.

The Influence of Stories from Others

We tend to take for granted not only the stories we create but also the ones that other people offer us, without questioning. Every day, you turn on the TV, look at the news on your smartphone, talk to your friends or parents. In each instance, you hear stories. You buy some and displace others. It's a daily and automatic process.

Stories Have the Power to Reinforce Existing Beliefs

We may think of our brain as impartial, but it is hardwired to be biased. It selects those bits of information that appeals to our existing beliefs and discards/ignores all others. Say you think the government is a mess. You watch TV and hear negative news about how the government is handling the economy. This story will reinforce your belief. You access your social media Apps, and some friends are complaining about the government. This will also reinforce your belief.

In another example, say you are concerned with your high cholesterol. You scroll down the daily news on your smartphone and notice that a famous actor died from a heart attack. You click on the link and read the details of the story. Your concern about your health only increases.

Stories Influence Our Attitudes in Life

The impact of a story to you will be more significant if it involves a critical domain of your life. For instance, if politics is very important to you and you believe that the country is going in the wrong direction, you are most likely to spend your days in resignation, concern, impatience and anxiety. Other topics might be more important to you than politics. In this case, even if you think the government is wrongly handling the country, your attitudes won't be so influenced by it.

Let's say that you were raised in a family in which "asking for help" was a sign of weakness. You are now 45 years old, and you have never asked for help. You solve all the problems by yourself.

That is until one day your car breaks down, your mobile phone is not working, and the nearest station is miles away; you have no option but to step out of the car and ask for help. Eventually, a truck driver stops and gives a lift to the nearest gas station. You are safe, but feel miserable. Why? Because you had to ask for help and therefore you failed.

In reality, there's nothing wrong with you. Rather, it is your story that needs to be *upgraded*.

How about this:

Instead of

"Only the weak ask for help."

Consider:

"Asking for help is a sign of strength."

Imagine, from this simple paradigm change, what will be the impact on your emotional and mental health? How will you behave differently, see and do things you were not able to do before?

How Culture Shapes Our Stories

A young fish is swimming and finds an old and quiet fish. Trying to start a conversation, he asks, "How is the water?" The older one replies, "Which water?" He has been living in the water for so long that he couldn't notice that he is surrounded by water every day.

And, it's the same with culture. Being born in a particular country and having spent most of your life there, you don't even question some stories told and reinforced to you millions of times. But are these stories true? Are these facts? Or just particular ways of looking at things?

In Brazil, since I was born, I learned that the way we greet people is by hugging and kissing on the cheek. To me, this attitude seemed so natural that it became a fact, not a story. But when at 35, I moved to the US, where most people only say hello by shaking hand, I got myself thinking, *what should I do?* Well, I returned their gesture but still thought to myself, "They are so cold. How about a hug?".

Nobody is wrong here. What is driving a different attitude towards greeting others are different stories. In collective societies like Brazil, establishing relationships is usually the first step. In individual societies like the US, respecting one space is the way to a good start.

I am proud of my Brazilian culture, but I came to the conclusion that the stories offered to me are just a starting point to become the individual I want to be and to develop the life I want.

It's a starting point, not a dead end. I can look at the collective stories that the Brazilian society told me since I was born in 1980 and decide which serve me, which I want to displace, which ones I want to keep and merge with stories I learned from other cultures.

Remember;

You are in the driver's seat to create or accept the stories that serve you and respectfully decline those that don't.

Exercise

Select a topic that you want to talk about. A particular issue that is making you overthink or suffer.

Step 1

Write down one sentence that defines your problem.

Step 2

Now write down the beliefs, stories and words that are coming to you every day and reinforcing this problem:

Step 3

From what you just wrote, separate stories from facts.

Step 4

Reflect on which stories you need to **displace** and what new stories you need to **accept** to change your relationship with this problem.

Example

Issue: "I don't have time to take care of myself"

What I keep telling myself and reinforces this problem:

a. "I drive 2 hours to work every day"

b. "Welcome to adult life"

c. "I have 3 kids"

d. "I need to be home every day at 6 pm to take care of the family"

Stories: b, d

Facts: a, c

Next steps: replace stories *b* and *d* with other stories that will help you to achieve your goal (have more time to take care of yourself).

Chapter 14
Conversations

Another transformational tool we use daily but tend to undervalue is the power of conversations. By 'conversations,' I am not referring to information exchange like asking other people what time is it or how's the weather forecast. That is not a conversation but rather a dialogue (sometimes a monologue ☺).

For a true conversation to take place, we need to pay attention not only to the *content* but specially to the *context*.

1. **Content:** the subject (s) we will discuss;

2. **Context:** how we will talk (live, virtual, over the phone), how much time do we have, and more importantly, in which emotional state we will have a conversation.

The Power of Conversations

Conversations can be powerful means of transformation; they literally create possibilities for the future. If your conversations are always the same, your future will likely be the same. For example, if Mary is unhappy with the way she has been treated by her boss, but all conversations they have are centered on "get things done" at work, the relationship between Mary and her boss is unlikely to change.

Until one day, Mary decides to move the course of the conversation, and instead of discussing her projects' status, she brings up the way she has been treated at the company. Without going too deep into the possible scenarios, this conversation is bound to open new doors. It will create a different type of relationship between Mary and her boss. A different future.

The Lack of Conversations

Many of the problems we face result from the lack of conversations. While we are addicted to conversations with the goal of produce something (i.e., check on projects' status), we lack so many critical conversations. Such as:

- Conversations about HOW we want to work together. How we will treat each other;

- Conversations about the purpose of what we are doing (What is the true value of what we are creating? Are we leaving a legacy?);

- Conversations about our values, what is important to us;

- Conversations about our differences;

- Conversations about what we want to change or stop doing;

- Conversations to explore possibilities. To dream, wonder and imagine scenarios together.

This list could continue, but I would like to invite you to think about which conversations are missing in your life.

Exercise

1. Reflect on which conversations you are having

    a. What are the objectives of these conversations?

    b. Which results are they leading to?

    c. How satisfied are you with the results you are achieving?

2. Reflect on which conversations are missing in your life (personal and professional)

    a. List the type of conversations you are missing

    b. Are these conversations missing with some people in particular? Who?

    c. Why are these conversations missing?

3. Select 1 conversation that you want to have in the next 7 days

    a. Plan for your conversation. Establish the objectives, content, and how it will happen (context)

b. Think about who needs to be part of this conversation

c. Reflect on the emotional states discussed early in the book (resentment, resignation, peace, and enthusiasm). In which emotional state do you need to be for this conversation? In which emotional state would you like the other participants to be?

d. If you think the participants won't be in the emotional state necessary for this conversation, does it need to happen now? If yes, what can you do to shape their emotional state?

Chapter 15
Body Practices

Among the most common behaviors I observe in my clients is the neglect of the body as a domain for personal transformation.

This is not their fault; it's just a reflection of how they were raised, surrounded by parents and teachers who always emphasized mind skills over body practices or emotional intelligence.

Although in the last decades we have made significant progress towards understanding our emotions (the publication of *Emotional Intelligence* by Daniel Goleman in the 1990s was a critical step in this direction), we are still trapped in the beliefs that successful careers and happy lives depend mostly on the development of our mental faculty. Think about how much time you spend every day reading, looking at screens, reflecting, overthinking, and how much you attach the development of your kids or loved ones to those skills.

The Immense Potential of Body Practices

If you ever practice sports, pay attention to the type of thoughts you have afterward. How contrasting are those thoughts versus the ones you had before the exercise?

In the minutes following a bike ride, few miles running, or any other sports practice done with focus and dedication, the thoughts, emotions, and energy that flows through your body are entirely different. Your body is now influencing how you OBSERVE your life, allowing you to perceive things you were previously not able to "see." Research shows that physical activity promotes all kinds of healthy changes in our consciousness, generating new activity patterns and releasing chemicals that energize, calm your spirit and restore clarity. This "enhanced vision" can lead you to different ACTIONS and RESULTS. This is a simple example of how the body can transform your reality. Therefore, it's no surprise that many people claim they have great ideas after their sports practice or while they are taking a relaxing shower.

Sports are a great way to activate the body and trigger new thoughts and emotions as well as fight off negative ones. On top of that, you can design an infinite number of individual and collective practices with the body. The following exercises showcase how to do that:

Exercise

1. Define one topic/challenge you are dealing with

2. Ask yourself: how is this challenge manifested in my body?

3. Stand up, move around your room or open space and embrace this challenge in your body. Where are you feeling this problem? In your belly, shoulders, face? Just feel it. Don't judge

4. Now think about the opposite of this challenge. For example, if you are feeling sadness, let's embrace joy.

5. How can you represent joy in your body? Walk around and try new movements. Stretch your body, walk in a different way, breathe in at a different pace. Continue to shape your body to embrace joy (if you feel lost and don't know how joy manifests in you, think about a friend that lives in joy. How he/she walks? How his/her body moves? Try to imitate their movements into your body)

6. Pay attention to how joy is manifesting in you. Where do you feel joy? Just pay attention, don't judge

Repeat this exercise daily for at least one month. Write down your insights in a journal, noting down the things happening with you: How are you looking at life? Which options do you have? What are the perspectives? Which thoughts are you having? Which emotions? What's your emotional state? How is the energy in your body?

Chapter 16
Transcendent Practices

Spirituality and transcendent practices such as meditation hold immense potential for us to unlock our best versions. Unfortunately, due to the confusion between spirituality and religion, many people simply avoid this life aspect.

Whereas religion is restricted by adherence to particular sets of beliefs, worldviews, practices, and behaviors, spirituality encompasses a multitude of beliefs, values, and practices. One doesn't need to follow a religion to be a spiritual person.

A new way of looking at spirituality is through the lenses of COHERENCE, the concept we discussed previously. When what you **feel** is aligned with what is you **think** and with your **body disposition**, you are in **coherence** – in a state of peace, gratitude, joy, and enthusiasm. One's impact on others and in the world around will be very different from when there's a lack of coherence.

Transcendent practices can be extremely powerful even in the most mundane of situations. For example, I usually make a short declaration before I join important meetings. This helps me to bring back my purpose (why I am here) and reestablish the coherence lost in the middle of a busy day.

"I can't do it"

One major reason why many of us avoid transcendent practices is that we get attached to the narrative that we don't have time or can't concentrate for more than a few seconds. *If I can't do meditation because my mind continues to jump from thought to thought, why even bother trying?*

In my experience, adopting these practices is like starting anything new. In the beginning, it's not easy. It takes us away from our comfort zone. We can't fully concentrate and don't feel the results. But as time goes by, as we persist, we start to get better, enjoy the process, see and feel the results. This is my invitation to you: look at a spiritual practice with openness and curiosity. Give time to see the results. They will come.

Reconnecting with Your Coherence Through Practice

Even if we try, nobody can stay in a state of coherence 24 hours a day, 7 days a week. Accept that practice moments exist to "bring you back to coherence" is an important step.

The following exercises will help you to reconnect with your coherence in the moments of need.

Exercise

The context (when, where, how) you do these practices is as important as the exercises:

1. Choose a place in your house where you will have silence, no distractions, and privacy;

2. To sustain the benefit of the practice over time, select one exercise of the list below and adopt it for at least 30 days;

3. Every day, practice at the same time (for example, 7 am) for a few minutes (5-15 minutes).

Examples of transcendent practices:

-   **Declarations:** as explained in the previous chapter

-   **Meditation**: although there are several types, I recommend the simpler method. Pay attention to your breathing. If thoughts come, don't get attached to them. Let them go

-   **Gratitude journal:** write down 3 things for which you are grateful for. Visualize these things and feel the gratitude in your body

-   **Do nothing and be present:** sit down for a few minutes and pay attention to yourself. How are you feeling? What are you thinking? What is your body telling you?

Chapter 17
Team Development

The Ontological approach can be highly effective for team development as well. Groups have the same opportunities and dilemmas as individuals. Although we see each other as separate entities with our own unique problems, we are, in many aspects of life, very similar.

Think about the breakdowns below. Do they apply to individuals or teams?

"I am not good enough. Others will always be better."

"I was never able to learn X."

"Others don't understand me. They don't know who I really am."

"I am confused. I don't know which path to take at this moment."

"I don't have time; I won't be able to finish this."

Clearly, they can be applied to both teams and individuals. Take, for instance, the first example: "I am not good enough. Others will always be better." This limiting belief can damage individuals, create pain and an infinite feeling of "lack of something." But it can also affect teams, producing an underdog feeling versus the competition and, by extension, poor results over time.

The Observer WE are

Due to the cultural beliefs prevalent today, most organizations and teams have a limited way to observe their work. Almost everything they do is observed through the lens of productivity, results, and speed to impact the customers.

"We only have value as a team if we produce fast, don't waste time and resources, and achieve our financial goals".

This example (or a variation of some sort) is usually the dominant narrative: a very narrow way of looking at performance and success. It's no surprise, therefore, that when we look at corporate executives and teams, they usually are in a resigned emotional state, disengaged, and lacking purpose.

Building High-Performance Teams

Using the Ontological approach to team development, we will start paying attention to the particular way the team observes. Diagnosis is the starting point and mostly happens without judgment, just paying attention to "what is." This phase involves questions like:

- What do they value?

- Why are certain things important?

- What is the team missing when they pay attention only to what's important to them?

- What are the narratives that sustain the team?

- Which narratives are producing the results they need and which are going against the desired results?

- What's the emotional state of the team? Are they working mainly from enthusiasm or resignation?

- How the team and its individuals "show up"?

- What is their leadership presence? When the team needs to bring up a project to the leadership, how are they perceived?

- The way the team "show up" is different when they interact with internal versus external customers? In which way? Does the way the team shows up demonstrates coherence or lack of coherence?

Note that these questions involve a full diagnosis of the OBSERVER the team is. Which set of beliefs (mind), emotions, and energy is dominating the team and affecting their performance and leadership presence. Once the diagnosis is made, we can progress with customized interventions that will allow the team and its individuals to see what is beyond their current paradigms. This expanded view will allow new actions that will drive better and consistent results.

Note that organizations continue to struggle year after year with a lack of employee engagement and innovation (just to mention two common topics). Why is that? Why we talk so much about these "problems" yet very little changes?

The methods we are applying to solve these "problems," focusing only on desired results and actions needed to get there, emphasizing only the domain of the mind, is insufficient. As Albert Einstein once said: "we cannot solve our problems with the same thinking we used when we created them." In ontological words, we need a different way to OBSERVE before we jump into ACTIONS...

Practices

<u>Meetings without agenda</u>

One way to avoid the trap of "being productive" and only focus on actions and results is to have a 'no agenda' meeting. Most people will feel uncomfortable with this proposal, thinking they are wasting their time. This is a normal reaction, so be ready to face some pushback from the team initially.

How to facilitate a meeting without agenda?

1. Open the meeting, stating that the objective is to create an open space to bring up HOW we are working together. "Today, I would like to invite you to focus on HOW we are working. We will leave the WHAT (i.e., projects status) for another meeting."

2. The meeting can flow with supporting questions (remember that sometimes questions are more important than answers) such as:

   - How are we really doing? What is going on in our professional (or even personal) lives? Anything you would like to share with the group?

   - What makes you proud?

   - Would you like to make a request to the team?

- What are things we need to start paying attention to?

- What are the things we need to start and stop doing?

3. At the end of the meeting and over the following weeks, ask for feedback from the participants. This will help you improve the flow of the next meeting, co-share the leadership with another person and bring topics that are specific to your organization and team

Facts versus Stories

Every time the team gets together to discuss a business result and what actions need to be prioritized, pay close attention to what has been said: are these facts, stories, or a combination of both?

As explained in Chapter 13, we have a tendency to quickly go over stories, treat them as facts, and jump into actions. It's, therefore, no surprise when these actions don't create the expected results.

To achieve the desired results, spend extra quality time on a good diagnosis based on facts (or stories closely related to facts).

Celebrity Body Practices

To bring emotions and body energy to a business meeting might sound crazy, but it is crucial for better performance. It's time to get rid of the old stories we have been telling ourselves and embrace the truth that our emotions and body energy play a huge role in individual and collective leadership.

1. Pay attention to the team's emotional and body state: are all or the majority of the individuals in a particular state? I.e.: "heads down and let's do the work," which can lead to resignation

2. Select one emotional state that the team will "play with." For example, dignity, joy, freedom, enthusiasm

3. Ask the team to think about a person that embodies this emotional state. Important that everyone in the meeting knows who this person is. It can be a person from within the company, but in this example, we will use a celebrity

4. Let's imitate this celebrity. For example, if it's Jim Carrey embracing joy, how does he walk, talk and speak? How he sits and remain silent? How would Jim behave in a business meeting? People might be reluctant to play this part of the game. Keep trying, and some will join you. Another way to bring people together is to change the celebrity and pick someone else the team suggested

5. Spend at least 5-10 minutes on Step 4. Then open for a round-robin of sharing. How did people feel? Which insights came to them? Was it easy or difficult?

With this practice, the whole team will feel a different

body energy that eventually will trigger new emotions and thoughts, beliefs, conversations. At the end of the practice, explain to the team the importance of having fun and playing with our body energy and emotions. Invite them to implement this exercise in their work routines. For example: How about sitting in my chair for the next 15 minutes if I were a king or queen? What is the energy that is coming to me? How would I behave?

Leadership Presence

Follow the steps mentioned above but instead of picking any emotional state and celebrity, focus on leadership presence: Is what I say aligned with what I feel and do? Who in our organization embraces this characteristic?

Let's imitate this person and see what our body and emotions can learn from her/him. How this person talks, walks, sits, and behaves? Why this person has such an impact on others?

Appendix
What Life is Trying to Teach Us?

In my childhood, I remember being a curious kid, one who loved to pay attention to things and ask why.

Being less than ten years old, on many Sundays, we used to drive back from the beaches in Sao Paulo State back to the city. I can still vividly recall lying down in the back seat of the 1980 silver Ford Corcel II my dad drove and spending the trip looking at the sky.

Picture 7 – In the back of a car like this, I started to wonder

"Why the sky is blue?", "What are the clouds made of?", "Why the clouds are moving?", "What exists out there, beyond the sky?" – these were the type of questions I asked myself.

I also remember that the road was surrounded by dense native rainforest. I used to imagine that extinct animals such as dinosaurs were still alive inside there, hiding deep within its misty, green confines.

Becoming an adult, with the busy life and responsibilities that come together, took me away from these wonders. I became too rational and occupied with thoughts and concerns about the future. The inner child in me vanished as I molded myself to the adulthood standards set by society.

But, in the last few years, particularly after my daughter was born, I noticed the curiosity, the childish wonder I had coming back. Since that transition, one of the main questions I have been asking myself is: What are the laws of life? What is life trying to teach us?

I don't see these questions limited to the domain of spirituality or religion. More and more, I am meeting people asking these questions, regardless of their spiritual beliefs.

Being now forty years old, I noticed some "lessons" that life has taught me. Some I have learned well, and others I'm still learning. I wonder how many more lessons are "out there" and I am not paying attention...

Regardless, here are the ones I see this "teacher" called life has to offer:

Free Yourself from The Need to Control

One of the biggest sources of pain I have noticed in myself and my clients is the illusion that we need to control everything. In this narrative, we are the powerful ones that shape life as we see fit. We try to control our careers, how our kids will behave, and where we want our life path to lead. *We choose what we want, and the World must obey. It is simple as that,* we like to think.

We want to believe we control our thoughts and emotions. "I choose to be happy, avoid sadness and any other bad emotions."

When we embrace this illusion, a World pandemic comes and flings us back into reality – **most of what happens in life we don't control.**

We don't control who our boss is going to be, if we will get along with him/her, what choices our kids will make when they are by themselves in the college room. And neither we control the experiences life has reserved for us (an accident, disease, or win the lottery).

Yes, there are several aspects of life we control, including the ability to make plans for the future. But, which percentage of our plans indeed became a reality? 50%, 30%?

Over and over again, life is trying to teach us that it is important to know the distinction between what we control (our choices) and what we don't. Do the best possible regarding what we control and be in peace with things we don't.

Are we learning the lesson? Or just becoming frustrated people that don't accept situations that life brings to us?

How are we educating our kids, siblings, friends? To design their lives to achieve only what they want and pursue the "happiness illusion" or to accept that frustrations are part of life and everyone will have to deal with them?

Live Fully in The Present Moment

The more we believe we control what happens to us and the surroundings, the more we tend to live in the future: making plans, projecting scenarios, daydreaming.

While we are in this future that never comes, life is happening. And we are not paying attention. We are not giving ourselves the chance to enjoy the present.

Nature does not make "plans." A Bear can reserve food for the winter, but that's it. It will never plan for a few years ahead. Only humans have this skill. And similar to other skills, if overused, it will most likely become a vice, not a virtue. Yes, planning for the future is vital. Notice what is happening with your life, make commitments and scenarios for the future. Continue to develop yourself and shape your desired future.

But also remember that you don't need to think about your future plans 15 times a day. Have a solid plan for the future but remember that the plan's execution will always happen in the present moment.

Many of us have (or had) pets. How about taking inspiration from them on living? One of the reasons animals enjoy life is that they are always in the present moment. The **now** is everything that is. If you leave your house for 1 minute and come back, your dog will receive you with the same excitement as if you were gone for a week. That's the magic of being fully in the present moment. The dog gives everything it has every second. No energy is spent worried over the future. No multi-tasking. No anxiety. Just the *Power of Now*.

You Are Enough

In this consumerist world we live in, this probably is the most difficult "lesson" for us to pay attention to. After all, every single day, we are bombarded by the narrative that we need this "new shiny toy" to be fulfilled.

You don't need more money to be happy. In fact, if you are reading this book, it is very likely money will not bring 1% more happiness to you. You already have the minimum necessary to live with dignity.

Whatever it is: buying a bigger house, having money for your dream vacation or a new car. Sure, all of this can make your life better but will not make you feel complete. After you achieve these things, the "next big thing" will shine and attract you.

Pursuing your dreams and goals is important, as long as you don't attach your value as a Human Being to those objectives. If you do, you will feel miserable while you don't achieve your dreams. Life is teaching us: the path to freedom (including financial freedom) is to accept who you are, what you have, and be grateful. Replace the beliefs that keep reinforcing the "lack of something" by narratives that show you are enough. You are a unique Human Being and you are enough.

Everything Is A Cycle

Picture 8 – Monk and his Mandala

I once heard the story that monks spend days building mandalas, beautiful works of art made of rock and sand. Once their hard work is finished, they destroy it. This is a way to remind them of the impermanence of material life.

But if we pay attention to the economic narrative that dominates the news, politicians' speeches, and corporate leaders' mindset, only growth matters. We need to pursue economic growth at all costs, even to the detriment of our environment and our future. After all, otherwise, we will never be rich and thus, happy.

Nonetheless, every once a while, an economic crisis comes from nowhere and reminds us that everything in life is a cycle of growth and decline.

Look at the seasons: winter, spring, summer, and fall. Every year nature is showing us the cycle of life and death. Everything in our life is a cycle. Of life, death, and reborn.

Are you willing to "let go" of old habits to create space for new ones? Replace old ideas, emotions and body postures with new ones. Finish a cycle of seeing your life in a particular way and start a new one when you are able to see with different eyes and pay attention to what you could not see before. Be in a new way.

The Journey Continues

We are all on this journey together. I wish all the peace, joy, and possibilities in your life. Take care of yourself to be able to take care of others.

It was a pleasure sharing this journey with you and I hope our paths cross again in the future.

Where to Learn More

You can find more about the topics discussed here at:

Websites

- Ontology, Personal and Professional Development - www.newfieldnetwork.com

- Positive Psychology - https://ppc.sas.upenn.edu

- Minimalism - www.theminimalists.com

- Anthroposophy (The 7-year cycles of life) - https://anthroposophy.org
- School of Emotions - https://schoolofemotions.world

Books

- Flourish: a visionary new understanding of happiness and well-being, by *Martin Seligman*
- The Power of Now: a guide to spiritual enlightenment, by *Eckhart Tolle*
- Man's Search of Meaning, by *Viktor Frankl*
- Mastery: the keys to success and long term fulfillment, by *George Leonard*
- Biographical work: the anthroposophical basis, by *Gudrun Burkhard*

Connect with Me

I offer individual and team development sessions using Ontological Coach, Positive Psychology, and other revolutionary methods.

You can find me here:

Website: www.danieldsantos.com

E-mail: contact@danieldsantos.com

YouTube: www.youtube.com/danieldsantos

Twitter: @DanielSantos1980

Instagram: @dsantos1980

COHERENCE

Made in the USA
Middletown, DE
22 November 2021

53137805R00076